DOMINOES

T0288633

The Three Musketeers

LEVEL TWO   700 HEADWORDS

OXFORD
UNIVERSITY PRESS

Great Clarendon Street, Oxford OX2 6DP

Oxford University Press is a department of the University of Oxford.
It furthers the University's objective of excellence in research, scholarship,
and education by publishing worldwide in

Oxford New York

Auckland Cape Town Dar es Salaam Hong Kong Karachi
Kuala Lumpur Madrid Melbourne Mexico City Nairobi
New Delhi Shanghai Taipei Toronto

With offices in

Argentina Austria Brazil Chile Czech Republic France Greece
Guatemala Hungary Italy Japan Poland Portugal Singapore
South Korea Switzerland Thailand Turkey Ukraine Vietnam

OXFORD and OXFORD ENGLISH are registered trade marks of
Oxford University Press in the UK and in certain other countries

ISBN: 978 0 19 424887 7 BOOK
ISBN: 978 0 19 463967 5 BOOK AND AUDIO PACK

No unauthorized photocopying

Printed in China

This book is printed on paper from certified and well-managed sources.

ACKNOWLEDGEMENTS

Illustrations by: David A. Roach

The publisher would like to thank the following for permission to reproduce photographs: AKG-Images p59 (Execution of Charles I
/ Luyken); Bridgeman Images ppiv (Joan of Arc (c.1412-31), Gilbert, Sir John (1817-97)/Trustees of the Royal Watercolour
Society, London, UK), iv (Portrait of William Shakespeare (1564-1616) c.1610, Taylor, John (d.1651)/National Portrait
Gallery, London, UK), iv (Portrait of Cardinal de Richelieu (1585-1642), Champaigne, Philippe de (1602-74)/Musee des
Beaux-Arts, Rouen, France), iv (Louis XIII (1601-43), Champaigne, Philippe de (1602-74)/Prado, Madrid, Spain), iv (Anne
of Austria (1601-66) with her son Louis XIV (1638-1715), French School, (17th century)/Chateau de Versailles, France), iv
(Portrait of King Charles I (1600-49), Dyck, Sir Anthony van (1599-1641)/Private Collection/Philip Mould Ltd, London), 58
(Portrait of Charles I (1600-49), Dyck, Sir Anthony van (1599-1641)/Private Collection), 58 (Portrait of Oliver Cromwell
(1599-1658) 1649, Walker, Robert (1607-60)/Leeds Museums and Galleries (Leeds Art Gallery) U.K.), 58 (Portrait of Nell
Gwynne, c.1680, Lely, Sir Peter (1618-80)/Geffrye Museum, London, UK), 58 (Portrait of King Charles II (1630-85), c.1675,
Lely, Sir Peter (1618-80)/Private Collection/Philip Mould Ltd, London), 59 (The Dashing Cavalier, Lomax, John Arthur
(1857-1923)/Haynes Fine Art at the Bindery Galleries, Broadway), 59 (Puritan, Roundhead, Pettie, John (1839-93)/Sheffield
Galleries and Museums Trust, UK/Museums Sheffield), 59 (John Milton, Faithorne, William (1616-91)/Huntington Library
and Art Gallery, San Marino, CA, USA/The Huntington Library, Art Collections & Botanical Gardens), 59 (Self Portrait with
a Sunflower, after 1632, Dyck, Sir Anthony van (1599-1641)/Private Collection/Philip Mould Ltd, London).

Cover: Ilian Stage courtesy of Alamy Images

DOMINOES

Series Editors: Bill Bowler and Sue Parminter

The Three Musketeers

Alexandre Dumas

Text adaptation by Clare West

Illustrated by David A. Roach

Alexandre Dumas was born near Paris in 1802. His grandmother was a Haitian slave, and his father, a general in the French army, died when Alexandre was only four. As a child, Dumas was poor, and had little education, but when he was twenty he went to live in Paris and soon became successful both as a playwright and a novelist. His most famous books, *The Three Musketeers* (1844) and *The Count of Monte Cristo* (1845) are both available in the Dominoes series. Alexandre Dumas died in 1870. His son, also called Alexandre, was a successful novelist, too.

OXFORD
UNIVERSITY PRESS

BEFORE READING

1 The story happens in the seventeenth century. Which people are you going to read about? Tick the boxes.

a ☐ — *Joan of Arc* FRENCH LEADER

b ☐ — *William Shakespeare* ENGLISH WRITER

c ☐ — *Cardinal Richelieu* PRIME MINISTER OF FRANCE

d ☐ — *Louis XIII* KING OF FRANCE

e ☐ — *Anne of Austria* KING LOUIS XIII'S WIFE AND QUEEN OF FRANCE

f ☐ — *Charles I* KING OF ENGLAND

2 Which of these things do you think you will read about? Tick the boxes.

a ☐ Men and women falling in love.

b ☐ People fighting.

c ☐ People sailing to America.

d ☐ People escaping from prison.

Chapter 1
D'Artagnan meets the three musketeers

The **Captain** of the King's **musketeers**, **Monsieur** de Tréville, sat back in his chair and looked with interest at the young man in front of him. 'So you're the son of my old friend **d'Artagnan**!' he said. 'Now tell me, why have you left your village to come all the way to Paris?'

'I'm hoping to become one of the King's musketeers, **sir**,' said d'Artagnan. 'If a great man like you can help me—'

'I see a lot of young men like you, who want to become musketeers. It isn't easy. You have to show how **brave** you are. It's strange that you haven't brought a letter with you, from your father—'

'Sir, I had one, but a man stole it from me, when I stopped for some food at the town of **Meung**! A dark, well-dressed man.' Just then d'Artagnan gave a shout. 'Look, sir, there he is, outside your window! Excuse me, I must catch him!' And he ran out of the room.

De Tréville smiled and shook his head. 'What a wild young man! He'll be a good musketeer one day!'

On his way downstairs d'Artagnan **bumped into** a tall, good-looking musketeer. 'Sorry!' he cried, and ran on.

But the musketeer stopped him. 'You must say more than "Sorry" if you bump into me. I'm Athos, and I don't like your **behaviour**. Have you just arrived from the country?'

'What do you mean?' replied d'Artagnan. 'I *am* from the country, but I'm as good as you are!'

'We'll see about that,' said Athos. 'I'll fight you at twelve o'clock outside the church over there.'

'Right,' said d'Artagnan. 'I'll be there, don't worry,' and he ran off again, hoping to find the man from Meung. In

captain the leader of a group of soldiers

musketeer a soldier who fights with swords and guns

Monsieur /məˈsjɜː/ Mr

d'Artagnan /dɑːˈtænjɒn/

sir you say this when you talk to a rich or important man

brave not afraid of doing dangerous things

Meung /mɜːŋ/

bump into to hit someone with your body when you are walking or running

behaviour the way that you do and say things

'I'll be there!' his hurry he bumped into a second musketeer, called Porthos, and knocked his hat onto the ground. It was a fine, expensive hat, and Porthos was very angry.

'I'll teach you a lesson, young man!' he shouted. 'Meet me on the bridge at one o'clock! And bring your **sword**!'

'I'll be there!' d'Artagnan called back. Just then he saw a third musketeer in front of him, and a **lady's glove** on the ground at his feet. Without thinking he ran over and gave the glove to the musketeer.

'Does it belong to a friend, perhaps?' he asked, smiling.

'That's none of your business!' replied the musketeer angrily. 'I'll have to fight you for that! Meet me outside the theatre at two o'clock. My name's Aramis.'

Now d'Artagnan couldn't see the man from Meung anywhere, and he had to fight three musketeers, the bravest and best fighters in the country. But luckily for him, when

sword a long, sharp knife for fighting

lady a woman from a good family

glove a thing that you wear on your hand

Athos, Porthos, and Aramis heard that they were all fighting the same man, they decided to forget his behaviour. They saw how brave he was, and he soon became their friend. They even found a **servant**, called **Planchet**, for him.

꙳

A few days later, Planchet showed a visitor into d'Artagnan's room. It was **Bonacieux**, the **owner** of the house. He was looking very worried. 'Sir,' he cried, 'please help me! I don't know what to do! Yesterday someone **kidnapped** my wife!'

'Really?' said d'Artagnan, interested. 'Tell me more.'

'Well, she goes to the **palace** every day, because she works for the Queen. It was a dark, well-dressed man who kidnapped her—'

'Aha!' cried d'Artagnan. 'That sounds like the man from Meung! Go on.'

'You see, my wife knows all the Queen's secrets. She knows that very soon an important Englishman will visit the Queen – you won't tell anyone this, will you? – perhaps you know who it is—'

'The **Duke** of Buckingham?' asked d'Artagnan. Most people in Paris knew that Buckingham was in love with the French Queen.

'Shh! The walls have ears! Yes. And the **Cardinal**, the King's first **minister**, wants to show the King that his wife has a lover! So he sent one of his men to kidnap my wife and find out what she knows!'

'Leave it to me,' said d'Artagnan. 'I'll find your wife for you.'

꙳

Later d'Artagnan told the three musketeers about the kidnapping.

'Remember that the Cardinal's our enemy and that we must keep the Queen out of danger,' said Porthos.

'We'll be stronger than the Cardinal if we work together,'

servant a person who works for someone rich

Planchet /ˈplɒnʃeɪ/

Bonacieux /bɒnˈæsjə/

owner the person that something belongs to

kidnap to take someone away and keep them as a prisoner

palace a big house where a king lives

duke a very important man

cardinal a very important man in the Catholic church

minister an important person who helps the king

/mə'dɑ:m/ Mrs

said d'Artagnan. 'One for all, and all for one!' They shook hands on it.

※

That evening d'Artagnan was in his room upstairs, when he heard a woman hurrying down the street. He looked out of the window. 'Perhaps it's **Madame** Bonacieux,' he thought, 'and she's escaped!' She went into the house, and at once started screaming.

'She's in trouble!' d'Artagnan told himself. He ran downstairs and knocked down the front door. Inside there were three soldiers, holding the young woman a prisoner. It wasn't long before the three were running away, afraid of d'Artagnan's angry shouts and his heavy sword.

Now d'Artagnan was alone with Madame Bonacieux. He saw her beautiful face, and for the first time he knew that he was in love.

He knew that he was in love.

'Sir, thank you for what you've done!' she said warmly.

'It was nothing, Madame. Those men work for the Cardinal. They wanted to kidnap you again, I think. They want to know about the Queen's secrets. You're in danger here.'

'Where can I go? There's a plan – I need to be free—'

'I can take you to the house of my friend Athos. He's away tonight, so you'll be alone, and nobody will know you're there.'

'Then please, let's go there now.' She took his arm, and together they went to Athos's house, where d'Artagnan left her.

But later that night Madame Bonacieux went out. She walked quickly to a house in the next street, where the Duke of Buckingham was waiting for her. She took him through a secret door into the palace. The Queen came to meet them, looking more beautiful than ever. Buckingham could not stop himself from **kissing** her feet.

'Sir!' said the Queen. 'We cannot speak for long!'

'But how happy I am to see you, even if only for a moment!' said Buckingham.

'I must tell you now that we can never see each other again. There will be **war** between our two countries, and – and I am married!'

'But love is greater than that! For three long years I've loved you, I've thought of you and hoped that you loved me too!'

'I cannot give you any hope,' said the Queen, looking away. 'Go, sir! If they find you here, you will die! And I'll be very unhappy!'

'You do love me after all! Give me something to keep, something which belongs to you, and I'll go at once!'

'Very well, then. Take these **diamonds**, and think of me.' She gave him a small **wooden** box, and he kissed her hand many times.

'I'll see you again, my Queen!' he cried, leaving the room.

kiss to touch lovingly with your mouth

war fighting between countries and people

diamond a very expensive stone that usually has no colour

wooden made of wood

READING CHECK

Are these sentences true or false? Tick the boxes.

		True	False
a	D'Artagnan wants to work for the Cardinal.	☐	☑
b	D'Artagnan nearly fights with Athos, Porthos and Aramis.	☐	☐
c	Athos, Porthos and Aramis are soon d'Artagnan's friends.	☐	☐
d	Someone took Monsieur Bonacieux's daughter from his house.	☐	☐
e	D'Artagnan helps Madame Bonacieux.	☐	☐
f	Later Madame Bonacieux takes the Duke of Buckingham to meet the King of France.	☐	☐
g	The Queen gives the Duke her diamonds.	☐	☐

WORD WORK

1 Match the words in the hat with the pictures.

kiss sword gloves palace cardinal diamond

a palace

b ....

c ....

d ....

e ....

f ....

2 Use the letters in the gloves to complete these sentences about the story.

a Athos, Porthos and Aramis are m u_s_k_e_t_e_e_r_s.   *sukreete*

b D'Artagnan is very b _ _ _ _ . He isn't afraid of fighting three musketeers.   *erav*

c When d'Artagnan b _ _ _ _ _ _ _ _ Athos, Athos is angry.   *sump onti*

d Monsieur de Tréville is the c _ _ _ _ _ _ _ of the king's soldiers.   *nitapa*

e The musketeers are very good at fighting with s _ _ _ _ _ _.   *sdwro*

f Planchet is d'Artagnan's s _ _ _ _ _ _ _.   *tanver*

g The Cardinal is the King of France's first m _ _ _ _ _ _ _ _.   *tenisir*

h Someone has k _ _ _ _ _ _ _ _ _ _ Mme Bonacieux.   *pandipde*

i The Queen gives a w _ _ _ _ _ _ box to Buckingham.   *edono*

j Porthos is the o _ _ _ _ of a fine hat.   *ernw*

GUESS WHAT

What happens in the next chapter? Tick four boxes.

a ☐ We learn more about Monsieur Bonacieux.

b ☐ We learn more about the Cardinal's plans.

c ☐ D'Artagnan helps the Queen of France.

d ☐ D'Artagnan helps the King of France.

e ☐ D'Artagnan helps the King of England.

f ☐ D'Artagnan helps the Cardinal.

g ☐ The three musketeers arrive in England.

h ☐ Buckingham loses some of the diamonds.

Chapter 2
Diamonds for the Queen

*M*adame Bonacieux was too busy worrying about the Queen's secret to think about her husband. While Buckingham was kissing the Queen's hand, Monsieur Bonacieux was standing in front of the Cardinal. The little man was white and shaking. He knew that the Cardinal was as **powerful** as the King. 'He'll kill me if he wants to, and no one can stop him! Oh, why did I marry my wife? She's got me into all this trouble!' he thought.

But luckily, the great Cardinal wasn't angry with him at all. After a few questions about Madame Bonacieux, he said, 'My dear monsieur, I'm so sorry that my men had to bring you here. But we've had a most interesting talk. Perhaps you'll help me if I need you another time. Please take this bag of gold, and feel free to leave.'

Bonacieux loved money nearly as much as he loved himself. 'Oh sir!' he cried. 'Thank you, thank you, sir!' And when he was out of the room, he shouted as loudly as possible, 'Long live the Cardinal!'

The next day the Cardinal heard about the Queen's secret visitor from one of the palace servants. First he went to see the King. Then he called another person to his office. She was a beautiful, well-dressed woman, with long **blonde** hair and large blue eyes. It was Lady de Winter.

'Milady, do you remember the King giving the Queen twelve diamonds for her birthday? Well, now she's given them to her lover!'

Milady smiled coldly. 'How stupid of her!' she said.

'You must leave for England today. The Duke of Buckingham will want to wear the diamonds, I'm sure. So

powerful rich and important

blonde light yellow

8

you must get near him, at a dance perhaps, and steal two of the diamonds. Bring them back to me, and then we can show them to the King.'

'Leave it to me,' said Milady.

At the palace the Queen was speaking worriedly to Madame Bonacieux. 'The King's just told me that there'll be an important dinner in a week's time. He wants me to wear my diamonds, but I gave them to Buckingham! The Cardinal visited the King this morning – it's part of his plan to show the King that I have a lover! What can I do?'

'We must get those diamonds back at once, Madame. Don't worry, I know someone who will help us. Write a letter to the Duke of Buckingham, and give it to me. My friend will take it to London.'

Madame Bonacieux was thinking of that good-looking young man, d'Artagnan. 'He's very brave!' she thought. And when she told d'Artagnan about the Queen's letter, he was more than pleased to help. He loved Madame Bonacieux, and he loved his Queen.

'What can I do?'

safe in no danger

attack to start fighting

'Her secret is **safe** with me!' he cried.

The next day he called the three musketeers together.

'Friends, we must travel in secret to England,' he told them.

'Can't you tell us why?' asked Athos.

'The Queen needs our help. That's all I can say.'

'I'll buy a new sword for the journey,' said Porthos happily.

'There's no time for that,' said d'Artagnan, 'we leave at once. Now listen carefully. We'll ride together, and fight to the death if anyone **attacks** us. I'm sure that the Cardinal is going to send his men to stop us. I have a letter from the Queen in my pocket. If I die, the next man must take the letter and ride on. If he dies, the next man must take it, and so on. The letter must arrive safely in London.'

The four friends and Planchet rode out of Paris.

Half an hour later the four friends and Planchet rode out of Paris, their swords in their hands. They did not know that the Cardinal's men were following them. At Chantilly

three men attacked Porthos, and he had to stay there and fight them. At Beauvais someone shot Aramis from an upstairs window, and he was badly hurt and couldn't go on. Then at Amiens two men took Athos prisoner while he was asleep. 'That just leaves you and me, Planchet!' said d'Artagnan.

The two men sailed to England, bought new horses and rode to London. There they soon found the Duke of Buckingham's house. D'Artagnan asked to see the Duke, who took him into a **private** room at once.

'What have you come to tell me?' asked the Duke. 'You come from France. Has something happened to the Queen? Quickly!'

'She is well, sir,' answered d'Artagnan, 'but she is in great danger. She sends you a letter. Here it is.'

'A letter from the Queen!' Buckingham took it with shaking hands and read every word. He looked up at d'Artagnan. 'I must send back her diamonds with you. Here they are. I keep them with me at all times.' He took a wooden box out of his pocket and opened it. Suddenly he gave a cry. 'There are only ten diamonds! Two have gone!'

'Has someone stolen them, sir?' asked d'Artagnan.

'Yes, I remember now. I was wearing them last night, and I was dancing with Lady de Winter. She works for the Cardinal, I think. But don't worry, young man. My **jeweller** will make two more, which will look just like the others. Stay here tonight, and tomorrow I'll give you the box of twelve diamonds to take back to the Queen. Shake hands with me, d'Artagnan, you're a very brave man.'

And so the next day d'Artagnan and Planchet were on another ship, sailing back to France. On their way they had no more adventures, and they arrived safely home in the evening. That night d'Artagnan slept in his bed at Monsieur Bonacieux's house, with the Queen's diamonds in his hand.

private away from other people

jeweller a person who works with expensive stones

READING CHECK

1 Put these sentences in the correct order. Number them 1–10.

a ☐ The Cardinal asks Milady to get two of the diamonds from Buckingham.

b ☐ The King asks the Queen to wear her diamonds to a dinner.

c ☐ D'Artagnan gives the Duke of Buckingham a letter about the diamonds.

d ☐ D'Artagnan takes the box of diamonds back to the Queen of France.

e ☐ The Duke finds two of the diamonds have gone from their box.

f ☐1 The Cardinal questions Monsieur Bonacieux.

g ☐ Madame Bonacieux asks d'Artagnan to go to England.

h ☐ The Duke's jeweller makes two new diamonds to go in the box.

i ☐ The three musketeers help d'Artagnan leave France.

j ☐ The next day the Cardinal finds out about the Duke's visit to the Queen.

2 Match the first and second parts of the sentences.

a 'He's very brave,'   1 says Milady about the Queen.

b 'How stupid of her,'   2 says d'Artagnan about the Queen.

c 'She's got me into all this trouble,'   3 says the Queen about the King.

d 'Her secret is safe with me,'   4 says Monsieur Bonacieux about his wife.

e 'You must get near him,'   5 thinks Madame Bonacieux about d'Artagnan

f 'He wants me to wear my diamonds,'   6 says the Cardinal to Milady.

WORD WORK

Use the words in the box of diamonds to complete the sentences on page 13.

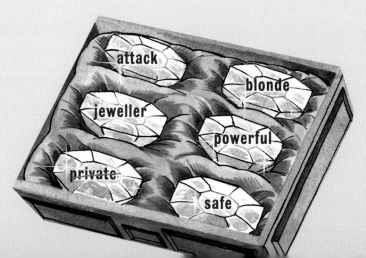

attack · blonde · jeweller · powerful · private · safe

a The Queen of France can only meet Buckingham in ...private...

b The Cardinal is a very .... man.

c Buckingham thinks the Queen's diamonds are .... but he is wrong.

d Milady has blue eyes and .... hair.

e Buckingham pays his .... to make two new diamonds to go in the box.

f The Cardinal's men .... the musketeers.

GUESS WHAT

What happens in the next chapter? Tick three boxes.

a ☐ D'Artagnan gives the diamonds to Madame Bonacieux.

b ☐ D'Artagnan gives the diamonds to Milady.

c ☐ The King is angry with the Queen.

d ☐ The Cardinal's men take the diamonds from Madame Bonacieux.

e ☐ The Queen wears the diamonds one evening at a party.

f ☐ The King is angry with the Cardinal.

Chapter 3
A second kidnapping

Very early the next morning d'Artagnan went to the palace to find Madame Bonacieux. He gave her the small wooden box, and she hurried happily away to give it to the Queen.

That evening everybody in Paris was talking about the dinner at the palace. Hundreds of important people waited in the great dining room for the King and Queen to arrive. First came the King, richly dressed, but looking very angry. Next was the Cardinal, looking **proud** but worried. And last, the Queen, looking beautiful, but tired. The King and Cardinal were some way away from the Queen, so they couldn't see her very well. Both of them kept their eyes on her dress. She was wearing the diamonds, but it wasn't easy to count them.

'Are there ten or twelve?' the Cardinal asked himself. He was playing a dangerous **game**, and he knew it. 'I've told the King that two are **missing**. Milady's given me the two diamonds stolen from Buckingham. So how can there be twelve on the Queen's dress?'

Suddenly the King called across the long table to the Queen, 'I am sorry that you're not wearing all my diamonds, Madame.'

The Queen lifted her beautiful head proudly. 'I don't know what you mean, sir,' she said. And she turned to him. The King and the Cardinal counted twelve diamonds on her dress.

'Well, Cardinal,' shouted the King angrily, 'what's all this about? Are you laughing at me? Explain yourself at once!'

'I'm sorry, sir,' replied the Cardinal. 'I – I made a mistake.'

The Queen smiled secretly to herself. And so did

proud feeling that you are more important than other people

game a secret plan or way of playing with other people's feelings

missing not there

d'Artagnan. He was the only one in the crowd who knew what was happening.

Just then he felt a woman's hand on his arm. He looked down and saw a letter on the ground. The woman was moving away, but he knew that it was Madame Bonacieux. He took up the letter, opened it and read it. It said:

> I'd like to thank you for what you've done. Come to the little house at the end of Avenue **Saint Cloud** at ten o'clock tomorrow night, and wait outside for me.
>
> Constance Bonacieux

The next evening he rode excitedly through the dark streets to the Avenue Saint Cloud. It was a quiet and lonely part of Paris, and even brave d'Artagnan started to feel afraid. But he saw no one, and waited until eleven o'clock outside the little house. He began to feel worried. 'Why isn't she here?' he thought. 'What's happened?'

Then he saw an old man walking slowly past. 'Excuse me!' said d'Artagnan. 'Have you seen a young woman go into this house?'

The old man looked afraid. 'If I tell you, perhaps the Cardinal's men will find out, and kill me!'

'Oh, so his men were here, were they?'

'That's right, sir, with a dark, well-dressed man. They took the young woman from the house and drove away in a **carriage**.'

'This is terrible!' thought d'Artagnan. 'The man from Meung has kidnapped the poor woman again! Is she hurt? Is she dead? How can I get her back this time? I know! I'll ask Athos what to do.'

He rode fast to Athos's house and woke up his friend. Athos listened carefully to d'Artagnan's story.

Saint Cloud
/sæŋ kluː/

carriage an old kind of car that horses pull

15

fall in love with
(*past* **fell, fallen**)
to begin to love
someone

shoulder this is
between your arm
and your neck

branded hurt by
a hot iron because
you did something
bad

hang to kill
someone by putting
something around
their neck and
holding them above
the ground

'Too late to do anything tonight,' he said, 'but tomorrow I'll ask Monsieur de Tréville to speak to the Queen about it. She'll find out where the Cardinal is keeping Madame Bonacieux prisoner.'

'Thank you. You're lucky that you've never been in love!'

'Do you think so? But I can tell you a love story, if you like. It's about a friend of mine, not me, you understand. Well, my friend was the head of one of the great French families. When he was twenty-five, he **fell in love with** a girl of sixteen. She was very beautiful, with long blonde hair and blue eyes. He married her and for a time they were very happy. Then one day, when they were riding together, she fell off her horse and hurt her arm. He ran to help her, and opened the top of her dress for her. There, on her **shoulder**, he saw that she was **branded**!'

'What a terrible story!' cried d'Artagnan.

'She was branded because she was a thief. He killed her – he **hanged** her from the nearest tree. That's why I never fall in love now.'

❧

D'Artagnan couldn't forget Athos's story. He was riding home, thinking hard, when he saw a carriage with a

beautiful blonde lady in it. She was talking angrily to a well-dressed Englishman. He was sitting on his horse and laughing at her.

'Can I help you, Madame?' called d'Artagnan. 'Is this **gentleman** being **rude** to you? I can teach him a lesson, if you like!'

Milady smiled up at d'Artagnan. 'Thank you, sir, but this gentleman is my **brother-in-law**, Lord de Winter.'

De Winter looked angry. 'This is none of your business, young man,' he said crossly. 'Kindly leave us alone!'

'No one speaks to me like that, sir,' replied d'Artagnan. 'Let's talk about this later, on the south side of the palace, perhaps?'

'Shall we say six o'clock? I'll be there,' said de Winter.

D'Artagnan's plan was to find out more about Milady. When, later that day, the two men met and fought, d'Artagnan won easily.

'I won't kill you,' he told de Winter, 'if you agree to take me to visit your **sister-in-law**. When I saw her today, I fell in love with her.'

Lord de Winter thanked d'Artagnan for **sparing** his life, and they agreed to meet at Milady's house the next day.

gentleman a man from a rich family who does not need to work

rude speaking loudly or crossly, using bad words

brother-in-law your wife's or husband's brother

sister-in-law your wife's or husband's sister

spare not to take

'Can I help you, Madame?'

READING CHECK

Match the first and second parts of these sentences.

a D'Artagnan gives the box of diamonds . . .

b There is a party at the palace . . .

c The Cardinal says that the Queen . . .

d The Queen shows everyone . . .

e Madame Bonacieux asks d'Artagnan . . .

f The man from Meung kidnaps . . .

g D'Artagnan meets Milady . . .

h D'Artagnan and Lord de Winter . . .

1 that she is wearing all twelve diamonds.

2 is wearing only ten diamonds.

3 to meet her one night.

4 to Madame Bonacieux to take to the Queen.

5 Madame Bonacieux again.

6 for hundreds of important people.

7 fight together.

8 talking angrily with her brother-in-law.

WORD WORK

Correct the boxed words in these sentences. They all come from Chapter 3.

a The Cardinal is a very **prowl** man. _proud_

b What a **rode** man. He's always talking and he never listens to other people. ....

c She killed lots of people and so when they caught her, they **handed** her from a tree. ....

d I hurt my **boulder** yesterday and now I can't move my arm very well. ....

e They got into an old **marriage** and drove off. ....

f Two of the diamonds are **kissing** from their box. ....

g Come on! Don't play **names** with me! ....

h Don't kill me. Please **spade** my life. ....

i She was **branched** on her arm. ....

GUESS WHAT

What happens in the next chapter? Tick the boxes.

	Yes	Perhaps	No

a D'Artagnan falls in
   love with Milady.

☐ ☐ ☐

b Milady falls in love
   with d'Artagnan.

☐ ☐ ☐

c Milady meets a
   secret lover.

☐ ☐ ☐

d D'Artagnan falls in love
   with Milady's servant.

☐ ☐ ☐

e Athos is worried
   about Milady.

☐ ☐ ☐

Chapter 4
A dangerous woman

Milady was very kind to d'Artagnan when Lord de Winter took him to her house. The young man found her very beautiful, and he no longer thought so often of Constance Bonacieux. Every day for the next month he visited Milady. He began to think that she really liked him.

One day, when he arrived at her house, her **maid**, Kitty stopped him. She was a **pretty** girl, who always smiled at him.

'Can I speak to you in private, sir?' she asked.

'Of course, Kitty. What is it?'

'Come up to my room, sir, where no one can hear us.'

Together they went upstairs to her small bedroom. D'Artagnan looked around. 'Does that door open into Milady's room?' he asked.

'Yes, sir. You love Milady, don't you?' asked Kitty unhappily.

'Yes, Kitty, I'm wildly in love with her.'

'I'm sorry about that, sir, because Milady doesn't love you at all. Look at this letter.' And she gave d'Artagnan a letter to read. It said:

> You haven't replied to me, Count.
> Don't you love me? I'm waiting for
> you. Come at ten o'clock any evening.
> Lady Clarice de Winter

maid a woman who works in a rich person's house

pretty beautiful

count an important man

'Did Milady write this and ask you to take it to someone?' asked d'Artagnan.

'Yes, sir, the **Count** de Wardes. She's in love with him. I'm telling you this, sir, because – because I'm in love with you myself!'

'Aha!' thought d'Artagnan. 'Kitty's love for me will be useful. I can find out more about Milady from her.' He said nothing, but gave Kitty a kiss. They spent the evening talking, laughing, and kissing.

At midnight they heard Milady call 'Kitty!' from her bedroom. D'Artagnan jumped up and hid himself in a cupboard. Kitty ran into Milady's room, and d'Artagnan could hear their conversation.

'Monsieur d'Artagnan didn't visit you tonight, Milady.'

'He'll come tomorrow. I'm planning to **take my revenge** on him.'

'Don't you love him, Milady?'

'Love him? I hate him! Why didn't he kill Lord de Winter? When my brother-in-law dies, I shall have all his money!'

'And Madame Bonacieux? What happened to her?'

'Oh, her! She's just a woman from the back streets. The Cardinal and I are keeping her somewhere safe, don't worry.'

D'Artagnan was **horrified**. Milady, who looked so beautiful, was truly **evil**! He began planning to take his revenge on her.

The next day he visited Kitty and gave her a letter for Milady. It said:

> Lady de Winter, how lucky I am to win your love! I shall visit you this evening at ten o'clock.
> Count Robert de Wardes

'But you wrote this!' cried Kitty.

'Yes, and tonight I'll visit Milady at ten. It'll be dark in her room, and she'll think that I am the Count de Wardes. Perhaps then I can find out what has happened to my poor Constance.'

In the end Kitty agreed, and d'Artagnan's plan worked

take your revenge to hurt someone who has hurt you

horrified very surprised and afraid

evil very bad

well. He spent the evening with Milady, talking softly of love and kissing her beautiful face in the soft orange light that came from the fire. Before he left, Milady took his hand. 'Oh Count,' she said, 'I'm so happy that you love me! Take this ring, and then you'll never forget me!' She put a diamond ring on the young man's finger.

The next morning d'Artagnan went to see his friend Athos, and told him all about his visits to Kitty and Milady. But Athos was more interested in the ring. 'Where did you get this?' he asked.

'Beautiful, isn't it? It's a present from Milady.'

'That's strange,' thought Athos. 'It looks like a ring that belonged to me once. I gave it to the woman who loved me, I thought. How stupid I was!'

Athos didn't speak for a moment. 'You're my friend, d'Artagnan,' he said. 'Listen to me. Forget about Milady. I don't know her, but I know that she's evil and dangerous. Keep away from her.'

D'Artagnan knew that Athos was right, but it was difficult to think of never seeing Milady again. He visited her that evening.

'Milady, I saw the Count de Wardes today,' he said.

'The Count?' Milady's face changed colour. 'Did you? Er . . . what did he say? Did he . . . speak of me?'

'I'm sorry to say that he was showing everybody your ring. He was laughing at you. A true gentleman is never so rude to a lady!'

Milady was white and she was shaking. 'He – he laughed at me? Me! D'Artagnan, that man is now my enemy! Fight him for me!'

'I'll be happy to kill him for you, Milady!'

'If you do that, we can be happy together, you and I.' She smiled, and took his hand. She let him kiss her again and again.

D'Artagnan forgot Athos's words, and he forgot Constance. He thought that Milady loved him, and so he said, smiling, 'You know that it was really me here in your room last night!'

'What do you mean?' asked Milady, pulling away from him.

'It wasn't the Count de Wardes who came to visit you, it was me.'

'Is that true? You'll be sorry for playing games with me, young man!' And angrily she attacked him, pulling out his hair and hitting him hard. D'Artagnan held her away from him. Just then her dress fell off her shoulder, and he was horrified to see that she was branded!

'I'm going to kill you!' she screamed wildly, holding a knife in her hand. The young man ran downstairs and into the street.

He was horrified to see that she was branded!

READING CHECK

1 Are these sentences true or false? Tick the boxes.

		True	False
a	De Wardes gives Kitty a letter for Milady.	☐	☑
b	Milady knows at once that the Count de Wardes who visits her is really D'Artagnan.	☐	☐
c	Athos thinks that he has seen Milady's ring before.	☐	☐
d	Milady wants d'Artagnan to fight de Wardes.	☐	☐
e	At the end of the chapter, Milady loves d'Artagnan.	☐	☐

2 Correct nine more mistakes in the chapter summary.

Constance Bonacieux

D'Artagnan forgets the Queen and goes to see Milady every day for a year. Milady has

a pretty maid called Kitty. Kitty tells D'Artagnan that Milady is in love with de Tréville.

Kitty herself is in love with Aramis. She shows him a letter from de Wardes. D'Artagnan

goes to visit Milady one morning saying that he is de Wardes. Milady gives him a gold

ring. Porthos is very interested in this ring. He tells d'Artagnan to be careful with

Milady. D'Artagnan tells Milady that he, and not de Wardes, visited her. Milady is very

happy with d'Artagnan. In the fight that they have, d'Artagnan sees that Milady's leg is

branded.

ACTIVITIES

WORD WORK

Find words in the flowers to complete the sentences.

a Kitty is Milady's m <u>aid</u>.

d She is in love with the C _ _ _ _ de Wardes.

b She is a p _ _ _ _ _ young woman.

e D'Artagnan is h _ _ _ _ _ _ _ _ by Milady because she is very bad, but he is interested in her too.

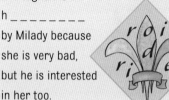

c Milady is an e _ _ _ woman who smiles a lot.

f Milady wants to take her r _ _ _ _ _ _ on d'Artagnan because he didn't kill Lord de Winter.

GUESS WHAT

What happens in the next chapter? Tick the boxes.

		Yes	No
a	Athos learns that Milady was once his wife.	☐	☐
b	The Cardinal wants to give d'Artagnan a job.	☐	☐
c	D'Artagnan agrees to work for the Cardinal.	☐	☐
d	D'Artagnan and the three musketeers go to fight the English.	☐	☐
e	The Cardinal sends Milady to kill Buckingham.	☐	☐
f	Milady wants to kill d'Artagnan.	☐	☐
g	Athos speaks to Milady.	☐	☐
h	Athos kills Milady.	☐	☐

Chapter 5

Meetings with the Cardinal

D'Artagnan ran all the way through Paris without stopping. When he arrived at Athos's house, he ran at once into his friend's bedroom.

'What's happened?' cried Athos, sitting up in bed. 'Is the King dead? Or have you killed the Cardinal? Tell me! You look terrible!'

'Are you ready for this, Athos?' said d'Artagnan, falling on to a chair. 'Milady's shoulder is branded!'

Athos put his hands over his face. 'Oh no! Surely she isn't . . .'

'Are you sure that your friend's wife – your wife – is dead? Milady's about twenty-eight, blonde with blue eyes.'

'It's her, I think! I must see her, d'Artagnan!'

'Don't go near her, Athos! You nearly killed her once, and she'll want to take her revenge. I'm afraid that I've made a terrible enemy in that woman – an enemy for us both!'

'You're right,' said Athos. 'We must both be very careful for the next two days. After that we'll be with the army, fighting the English. And then it won't matter if it's Milady or the English army who kills us!'

When d'Artagnan went back to his room, Planchet gave him a short letter from the Cardinal.

The Cardinal asks Monsieur d'Artagnan to visit him this evening at eight o'clock.

'Hmm,' said d'Artagnan. 'What's the Cardinal's plan? Perhaps he'll put me in prison! But I will go to see him. I can always take my friends with me.'

That evening Athos, Porthos and Aramis waited outside the Cardinal's palace, while d'Artagnan went in for his meeting. The great man was alone in his office when d'Artagnan walked in.

'Ah, d'Artagnan. I've heard a lot about you. You had some special business in England a few weeks ago, I understand?'

'You know about that, sir?' asked d'Artagnan.

'My **spies** are everywhere. I haven't **punished** you yet . . .'

'That's very good of you, sir.'

'. . . because I can see that you're brave and **intelligent**. And I have a job for you, d'Artagnan. Would you like to be a captain in my army?'

'Sir, that's very kind of you, but . . .'

'Well, man, come on, come on! Give me your answer!'

'. . . I'm going to become a King's musketeer, sir.'

'There's no difference between my soldiers and the King's,' replied the Cardinal coldly. 'But I see that you want to stay with your friends. Soon the war between France and England will begin, and many soldiers will die. If you are still alive after the fighting, I'll ask you about this again. Goodbye, young man.'

When d'Artagnan told his friends about this conversation, they all agreed he was right to say no to the Cardinal. But d'Artagnan knew that the Cardinal was **warning** him to be careful.

The King's musketeers spent the next month fighting the English, who were in the French town of La Rochelle. D'Artagnan was fighting with his friends, and several times he had a lucky escape from death. He knew that his attackers weren't English soldiers, but Milady's men. Every night, before he went to sleep, he tried to think of a way of finding Constance and punishing Milady at the same time.

spy a person who tries to learn secret things

punish to hurt someone because they have done something wrong

intelligent quick-thinking

warn to tell someone about danger or about a bad thing that may happen

One evening Athos, Porthos, and Aramis were on **guard duty** outside the town. They saw a carriage drive up to an **inn**. A lady got out and went into the inn. Soon afterwards a gentleman arrived, got off his horse, and went in. Lights went on in the lady's room.

'That man looked like the Cardinal!' said Aramis.

'And that woman looked like . . . Milady!' said Athos. 'Let's go nearer and listen to what they're saying.'

Luckily the window was open, and the three musketeers could hear every word of the conversation.

'This is very important, Milady,' said the Cardinal. 'You must go at once to England, to see Buckingham. Tell him that if the English go on attacking France, I'll tell the world about him and the Queen.'

'But what if he doesn't listen, and goes on attacking us?'

'An intelligent woman like you can find a way of stopping him.'

'Ah, I understand. Well, sir, a man for a man, a life for a life, help me to kill my enemy and I'll help you to kill yours!'

'Who is your enemy, Milady?'

guard duty
watching out for
the enemy

inn an old name
for a hotel where
you can eat, drink,
or stay

28

'That evil little d'Artagnan! He must die!'

'Do what you like with him. I'll give you a letter to say that you're free to punish him in any way.'

The musketeers could hear every word.

The Cardinal gave Milady a piece of paper and left the room. The musketeers hid behind a wall and watched him ride away.

'Follow him and see where he's going,' Athos told Aramis and Porthos. 'I'll stay here for a while.' The two friends rode off after the Cardinal, and Athos went into the inn. He walked at once into the lady's room without knocking.

'Who are you? What do you want?' cried Milady, afraid.

'Yes, it's her,' Athos said to himself. He took off his hat and walked up to her. 'Do you know who I am?' he asked.

Milady went deathly white. 'Yes – yes, I do!' she cried.

He put his gun to her head. 'Evil one! I know that you're the Cardinal's spy, and I know what you're planning! But d'Artagnan's my friend! If you hurt him, I'll kill you! Give me the Cardinal's letter!'

With a shaking hand she gave it to him, and he left the room.

READING CHECK

1 Correct the mistakes in these sentences.

a D'Artagnan tells ~~Porthos~~ *Athos* about Milady's shoulder.

b The King sends a letter asking d'Artagnan to visit him at eight o'clock.

c The Cardinal asks de Tréville to be a captain in his army.

d The musketeers and d'Artagnan go to fight the Germans in La Rochelle.

e Milady's men attack Athos several times.

f The Cardinal asks the Queen to speak to Buckingham.

g The Cardinal gives Milady a letter saying that she can punish Buckingham in any way.

h The musketeers listen to the Cardinal talking to Athos.

i Aramis takes the Cardinal's letter from Milady.

2 Who says this? Who do they say it to? Choose from the names below.

a ☐ 3 'I've heard a lot about you.'

b ☐ 'I'm going to become one of the King's musketeers.'

c ☐ 'Milady's shoulder is branded.'

d ☐ 'Who are you? What do you want?'

e ☐ 'Evil one!'

f ☐ 'Help me to kill my enemy and I'll help you to kill yours.'

1 D'Artagnan to the Cardinal

2 Milady to Athos

3 the Cardinal to d'Artagnan

4 Milady to the Cardinal

5 D'Artagnan to Athos

6 Athos to Milady

WORD WORK

Use the words in the hat to complete the sentences.

a Milady and the Cardinal meet in an
inn .

b Milady is the Cardinal's ....

c The Cardinal is an evil but
.... man.

d He decides not to ....
d'Artagnan for working for the Queen.

e The Cardinal .... d'Artagnan
not to work against him any more.

f The three musketeers are on ....
.... in La Rochelle when Milady arrives.

*spy inn
punish
warns guard duty
intelligent*

GUESS WHAT

What happens in the next chapter? Tick the best answers.

a Why are the three musketeers worried?

1 ☐ Because the Queen is ill.

2 ☐ Because Milady wants to kill
d'Artagnan.

3 ☐ Because the English are going to
attack La Rochelle.

b What do the musketeers do while the
English are getting ready to attack?

1 ☐ They eat and drink.

2 ☐ They run away.

3 ☐ They get ready to fight.

c What happens to the Cardinal's letter?

1 ☐ The musketeers burn it.

2 ☐ The musketeers lose it.

3 ☐ The musketeers decide to put it
in a safe place.

d What do the musketeers do?

1 ☐ They write to the Queen
and to Lord de Winter.

2 ☐ They write to the King
and the Cardinal.

3 ☐ They kill Milady.

e What happens to d'Artagnan?

1 ☐ He goes to prison.

2 ☐ He dies.

3 ☐ De Tréville wants him to
be a musketeer.

Chapter 6 — A picnic in the castle

*W*hen d'Artagnan met the three musketeers the next morning, he saw that they were all looking worried. 'What's happened?' he asked.

'We'll tell you later,' said Athos. 'But first we need to find a safe place where we can talk. There are too many of the Cardinal's spies round here. Where can we go? I know! Let's have a **picnic** in the **castle** of La Rochelle! Our men drove the English away from it yesterday, so it'll be quiet now.'

'But the English will want to attack it again!' said Porthos.

'Well, if they do, then we can fight them,' replied Athos.

'And it is true that nobody will listen to us there,' said Aramis.

❦

So a few minutes later the four friends left the French **camp** and crossed a field, where dead bodies lay from the fighting of the day before. Then they climbed a hill to the castle. Behind them came Planchet, carrying a large, heavy **basket** of bread, meat, fruit, and some bottles of good **wine**.

'Here we are!' said Athos, when they arrived at the top of the castle. 'Up here we can easily see if someone's planning to attack us. Is breakfast ready, Planchet? I'm as hungry as a horse!'

They sat on the ground and started eating.

'Tell me your news, Athos!' said d'Artagnan. 'I must know what you've been doing!'

'It's important,' replied Athos. 'We saw Milady outside La Rochelle last night.'

D'Artagnan dropped his glass of wine. 'You saw Milady!'

'Who is Milady?' asked Porthos.

picnic a meal that people eat outside in the country, often sitting on the ground

castle a large old building with strong, high walls

camp a place where soldiers stay in tents for a short time

basket a box for carrying food

wine a red or white alcoholic drink made from grapes

'She's an evil woman who wants to take her revenge on d'Artagnan. Last night she asked the Cardinal to help her to kill him.'

'What?' cried d'Artagnan. 'Then there's no hope for me. My enemies are too powerful! I must get ready to die!'

'Forget about that for the moment,' said Aramis. 'Look down there! The English are going to attack the castle!'

'Well, I'm going to finish this wine and chicken first,' said Athos. He finished eating and drinking, then put down his empty glass, and took up his gun. 'Now, musketeers, let's show them!'

Bang! Bang! Two of the English soldiers fell. Bang! Bang! Two more lay dead, and soon the rest were running away very fast.

'More wine please, Planchet,' said Athos, sitting down again. 'Now where were we? Ah yes. The Cardinal is sending

'I'm going to finish this wine and chicken first.'

bang the noise a gun makes

33

Milady to England, to talk to, and possibly to murder, the Duke of Buckingham.'

'Murder him?' said d'Artagnan, horrified. 'But what can we do to stop her?'

'Well, to start with, I've taken the Cardinal's letter away from her. Here it is.' Athos put it on the ground in front of them. They all looked at it.

Nobody can punish the person who carries this letter for what they have done.

Richelieu

3 December 1627

'The owner of this letter is free to do anything! She can kill anyone she wants to,' said Aramis.

'Yes, so we must put this letter in a very safe place,' said Athos.

Just then Planchet called out, 'The enemy is attacking again!' Twenty English soldiers were running across the field towards the hill.

'Guns at the ready!' said Athos. 'Now!' Bang! Four soldiers dropped to the ground, and a few minutes later – bang! – three more fell. But the rest were now climbing up the hill towards the castle.

'Over here, all of you!' cried Athos, running to one of the castle walls. The wall was very old, and some of the stones were missing.

'Stand by this wall, and when I say "Push," push as hard as you can! You too, Planchet!' The five men pushed against the heavy wall, and it fell with a great crash on to the heads of the enemy. There were terrible cries, and then all was quiet.

Athos put an arm round d'Artagnan, who was looking

The five men pushed against the heavy wall.

down sadly at the dead men. 'It's war, you know, my friend,' he said. 'Perhaps it'll be us tomorrow! Now, gentlemen, we need to think of a plan.'

'Yes,' said Porthos. 'I'd like to kill Milady. We won't be safe while she's alive. She doesn't know me, so I can easily get near her.'

'Kill a woman!' cried Aramis. 'I don't like that. No, I have a much better plan. We must tell the Queen that Buckingham's life is in danger.'

'How will that help the rest of us?' asked Porthos.

'I know!' said Athos. 'Milady has an English brother-in-law, Lord de Winter. We can warn him that she's planning to kill Buckingham. Then he can watch her carefully, or even lock her up.'

'Wonderful!' cried d'Artagnan. 'Let's write two letters, then. One to the Queen, and one to Lord de Winter. Who'll write them?'

'Aramis is a good letter writer. He writes a lot of love letters,' said Porthos, smiling.

'I don't!' said Aramis. 'But I can write a good letter, it's true.'

An hour later, the two letters were ready. When Aramis read them aloud to the others, Athos said, 'Aramis, you're the king of letter-writers!'

'I'll send the Queen's letter to one of my friends,' said Aramis, 'who can give it to the Queen.'

'A lady friend, perhaps?' smiled d'Artagnan. 'And Planchet can take Lord de Winter's letter to England for us.'

delighted very happy

damage to break or harm something

❧

When the friends arrived back at the French camp, they found that Monsieur de Tréville was waiting for them.

'Everybody's talking about your brave fighting at the castle!' he said. 'D'Artagnan, I'd like you to become one of the King's musketeers at once!'

D'Artagnan and his three friends were **delighted**.

❧

While they were listening to this news, Milady was sailing to England. Unluckily for her, a storm **damaged** the ship that she was in. So her journey took her much longer than usual, and she arrived there on the same day that Planchet left England to go back to France. Lord de Winter had already read the letter from the musketeers.

So when Milady reached England, Lord de Winter's men were waiting for her. They took her to his castle, where they locked her in a room with a strong wooden door.

She was now a prisoner.

'I can write a good letter, it's true.'

37

ACTIVITIES

READING CHECK

Match the sentences with the people.

1 The Cardinal

2 Planchet

a Planchet carries food and wine for ..6..

b ...... and ...... push the castle wall onto the English.

c Athos tells the others about Milady's meeting with ......

d Athos tells the others that Milady is going to meet and perhaps kill ......

e Athos takes out ......'s letter for the others to read.

f Aramis writes two letters. One to ...... and one to ......

g ...... takes Lord de Winter's letter to England.

h ...... puts Milady in prison.

3 Lord de Winter

4 The Queen   **5** Buckingham   **6** The musketeers

WORD WORK

Find words in the road to complete the sentences.

a There is a c̲a̲s̲t̲l̲e̲ on the hill in La Rochelle.

b The musketeers decide to have a _ _ _ _ _ _ there.

c Planchet carries the _ _ _ _ _ _ with all the food and drink in it.

d They take some bottles of good _ _ _ _ with them.

e There are a lot of the Cardinal's spies in the French _ _ _ _ so they don't want to talk there.

f The musketeers are _ _ _ _ _ _ _ _ _ _ when they hear that d'Artagnan is going to be a musketeer.

g A storm _ _ _ _ _ _ _ _ the ship that Milady is travelling on.

h '_ _ _ _' is the sound that a gun makes when you shoot it.

GUESS WHAT

What happens in the next chapter? Tick the boxes.

a Milady leaves prison because she ☐ talks to Lord de Winter.
☐ escapes.

b Milady ☐ kills
☐ asks someone to kill Buckingham.

c ☐ The Queen
☐ The Cardinal sends a letter to Buckingham asking him to stop the war between England and France.

d Milady goes back to France and meets ☐ Constance Bonacieux.
☐ the Queen.

e Milady becomes Constance's ☐ friend.
☐ enemy.

Chapter 7 *Milady at work*

ilady looked round her room, horrified. 'Why has de Winter brought me here? Someone has told him of my plans! I must get out of here!' Just then the door opened, and a young army captain came in. Suddenly Milady was no longer afraid. 'Ah!' she thought, smiling to herself. 'Perhaps I can **persuade** him to help me escape!'

'Good morning, Milady,' said the young captain. 'I'm John Felton. Lord de Winter has sent me to **guard** you, day and night.'

'I understand, sir,' said Milady. 'I hope that I won't be any trouble to you. I've done nothing wrong, so I have nothing to fear from **God** or Lord de Winter. Leave me now. It's time for me to **pray**.' She closed her eyes, put her hands together, and **pretended** to pray.

John Felton left the room, looking surprised. 'Lord de Winter told me that she was evil!' he thought. 'Perhaps he's wrong!'

Every day for the next week, Felton visited Milady. Each time she pretended that she was praying, and did not look at him. In the end she looked up when he came in. He saw her beautiful face, and felt very sorry for her.

'Go on praying,' he said. 'God will look kindly on your crimes.'

'My crimes? Sir, you don't understand! It's other people who need God's help, not me! I am praying for them!'

'What do you mean, Lady de Winter?'

'I'll tell you everything, sir. This is what happened to me. When I was young and, unluckily, beautiful, a man fell in love with me. He kidnapped me and hoped to persuade me

persuade to make somebody change their way of thinking

guard to watch a prisoner and to stop him or her from running away

God an important person who never dies and who decides what happens in the world

pray to speak privately to God

pretend to try to make somebody believe something

to marry him. He found that he couldn't persuade me, so he began to **seduce** me, but I fought against him. "All right, I'll let you go!" he said angrily in the end. "You'll never love me, I can see that!"

"I'll tell the world that you kidnapped me!" I told him.

"But nobody will listen to you if they think that you're a criminal!" he replied. And with a hot **iron** he branded my shoulder!'

'Who was this evil man?' asked Felton, horrified.

'The – the Duke of Buckingham!' said Milady softly.

He saw her beautiful face, and felt very sorry for her.

seduce to persuade or to force someone to have sex with you

iron a metal stick which is used to burn someone

'And why is Lord de Winter keeping you a prisoner?'

'His brother fell in love with me and I told him my terrible secret. But he died soon after we married, so he didn't have time to tell Lord de Winter. I think that Buckingham has told de Winter to keep me here for a while, and then kill me or send me to Carolina for life!'

Felton kissed Milady's hand. 'You are an **angel**! Here's one man who will fight for you! I'll help you to escape! And, with God's help, I'll take revenge on Buckingham for you, too!'

Milady was delighted that her plan was working. That night Felton came quietly to her room and helped her to get out of the window. He climbed down to the ground, carrying her on his back. From there they ran across a field to the sea, where a ship was waiting for them.

Felton spoke to the ship's captain. 'Sail to Portsmouth,' he said. 'I have business there, so you must wait for me. Then when I'm back on the ship again, we can sail to France!'

At Portsmouth, a large town by the sea in the south of England, the English army was getting ready to attack France. There were hundreds of ships, full of soldiers, waiting for the Duke of Buckingham to tell them to sail. Buckingham himself was there, staying at one of the inns. Felton went to this inn. He asked to see the Duke at once, and the servant showed him into the Duke's room.

'Sir, I've come about Lady de Winter,' he told the Duke.

'That evil woman!' said Buckingham, angrily. 'But what are you—'

'Not evil, sir! She's an angel! You're the evil one! God will punish you because you kidnapped her! You seduced her! You branded her! And now you'll die for your crimes!' And Felton took out a knife and pushed it deep into Buckingham's **chest**.

angel a very good and beautiful person; in pictures they usually have wings

chest the top half of the front part of the body

'Patrick, help me, I'm dying!' the Duke called to his servant. At that moment Patrick ran into the room, saying, 'Sir, a letter from France!'

'Is it from the Queen?' asked Buckingham. 'Tell me what she says!'

'Sir, you're hurt! Let me call a doctor!' said the servant.

'No, it's too late. Tell me, Patrick! There isn't much time!'

'Sir, she says, "Please stop this war and **save** the lives of hundreds of English and French people. Be careful. Your life is in danger. Stay alive for the day when you are no longer my enemy."'

The Duke was losing blood fast. 'Is that all, is that all?' he asked with difficulty. 'Is there nothing more?'

'Sir, she says that she still loves you.'

'Thank God,' said Buckingham. 'Then my death will really mean something to her.' And smiling a last smile, he died.

When Lord de Winter arrived at his castle, he found out about Milady's escape. He rode as fast as he could to Portsmouth, but arrived just too late to stop Felton and save the Duke's life.

While Buckingham lay dying, Milady's ship was on its way to France. 'The English will catch Felton and hang him for murder, but he's done good work for me and the Cardinal,' Milady thought. 'When we arrive in France, I must go to **Béthune**. I hear that the Queen has moved that stupid little Bonacieux woman to the **convent** there.'

When Milady arrived at the convent, she asked to meet Madame Bonacieux, and was very kind to the lonely young woman. Soon the two women were spending most of their time together, and Milady pretended to be Constance's dearest friend. They talked about everything, and Constance told Milady how much she loved a young man called d'Artagnan, one of the King's musketeers.

save to take someone out of danger

Béthune /be'tju:n/

convent a church building where women (called nuns) live, work and pray; in the past, a convent was a safe place for a woman in danger

43

'He's coming here soon, you know!' she said excitedly.

'What? Here?' cried Milady. 'Impossible! He's at La
Rochelle!'

'So you know him as well, Milady! Is he – was he – in
love with you too? Tell me! I must know!'

'Oh no, I just know him as a friend.' Milady had to think
quickly. 'He told me all about you, the love of his life! So
now at last I've met you, dear Constance! How happy I
am!' And she held the young woman in her arms, smiling
lovingly at her.

One day a gentleman arrived at the convent and asked to
see Milady. He was Rochefort, one of the Cardinal's men,

and he came to give Milady a letter from the Cardinal. She asked him to send a carriage for her an hour later. When he left, he passed four men riding fast towards the convent. They were d'Artagnan and his friends.

'Look!' cried d'Artagnan. 'It's the man from Meung again!'

'He's dropped a piece of paper,' said Porthos. 'It says **Armentières**. That's a village near here, I think.'

'No time to follow him, gentlemen!' said Athos. 'Let's find Madame Bonacieux first!'

⚜

At the convent Milady was talking to Constance. 'Listen to me, my dear. We're both in great danger!'

'Oh dear! How do you know?' Constance looked afraid.

'The man who visited me just now was my brother. He told me that the Cardinal's men are coming to take us both away!'

'But d'Artagnan is coming to save me! He'll be here soon!'

'No, my dear, he isn't coming. The Cardinal's men will arrive dressed as musketeers and take us to prison, if we don't get away!'

'How terrible! Dear Lady de Winter, don't you have a plan?'

'I have, my dear. My brother's sending his carriage in half an hour, and I'm going off in it to hide somewhere a few miles from here. Why don't you come with me?'

'Very well. How good you are, Milady! Thank you!'

'Now, go to your room and pack any little things that you want to take with you – d'Artagnan's love-letters, for example.'

Constance hurried to her room, while Milady stood by the window, looking down at the road. 'Will Rochefort's carriage or the musketeers get here first?' she thought. 'Will I be able to stop d'Artagnan saving his Constance? What about my revenge? Let's see what happens!'

Armentières
/ɑːmɒnˈtjeə/

READING CHECK

Choose the right words to complete the sentences.

a Milady tells John Felton that . . .
kidnapped her when she was younger.
- 1 ☐ the Cardinal
- 2 ☑ the Duke of Buckingham
- 3 ☐ Lord de Winter

b Milady gets . . . to help her escape.
- 1 ☐ John Felton
- 2 ☐ Lord de Winter
- 3 ☐ the Cardinal

c . . . kills Buckingham.
- 1 ☐ John Felton
- 2 ☐ Milady
- 3 ☐ The Cardinal

d The Duke of Buckingham's servant Patrick brings him a letter from . . .
- 1 ☐ the King of France.
- 2 ☐ the Queen of France.
- 3 ☐ the Cardinal.

e Buckingham dies feeling . . .
- 1 ☐ happy.
- 2 ☐ sad.
- 3 ☐ angry.

f Milady goes to find . . . in Béthune.
- 1 ☐ the Queen
- 2 ☐ Constance Bonacieux
- 3 ☐ d'Artagnan

g Milady tells Constance that d'Artagnan is her . . .
- 1 ☐ cousin.
- 2 ☐ lover.
- 3 ☐ friend.

h Milady tells Constance that . . . are coming to take her away.
- 1 ☐ the musketeers
- 2 ☐ the Cardinal's men
- 3 ☐ the English

ACTIVITIES

WORD WORK

Use the words in the prison wall to complete Milady's diary.

angel	convent
~~guarding~~ iron	persuade
prayed	pretended	save
seduce		

It will not be hard to escape from this prison. Today I talked with Felton, the young man who is **(a)** ...guarding. me. Perhaps I can **(b)** .... him to help me. I **(c)** .... to be a very good woman and I said that I went to church and that I **(d)** .... there every day. I also told him 'Buckingham tried to **(e)** .... me when I was younger and he branded my shoulder with a hot **(f)** ....' After I finished my story Felton looked at me and called me 'an **(g)** ....'. When I escape from here, Buckingham will die. Then I will find Constance. I think she is living in a **(h)** .... in France now. I will use her to get d'Artagnan to come to me. Nothing and nobody will **(i)** .... d'Artagnan then. He will die in my arms!

GUESS WHAT

What happens in the next chapter? Tick the boxes.

a Milady kills ☐ Constance.
☐ d'Artagnan.

b ☐ Constance
☐ Milady runs away before the ☐ musketeers
☐ Cardinal's men arrive.

c ☐ Milady
☐ Constance dies in ☐ d'Artagnan's
☐ Athos's arms.

d The musketeers, d'Artagnan and de Winter go to find ☐ Milady.
☐ the Cardinal.

e In the end ☐ Milady
☐ The Cardinal must die.

Chapter 8 Revenge

When Constance came back into the room, Milady persuaded her to eat some chicken and drink a glass of wine. Suddenly they heard the sound of horses on the road. Milady ran to the window. She could see that the riders were the four musketeers. 'It's the Cardinal's men!' she said. 'Quick! We must escape through the garden! Follow me!'

But poor Constance could not move. 'Go without me, Milady!' she cried. 'Save yourself! I'm so afraid! I can't stand up!'

'Leave you here? Never!' replied Milady bravely. She opened the stone on her ring, and secretly put some **poison** from it into Constance's unfinished wine. Then she held the glass to the young woman's mouth, and with a smile, helped Constance to drink it. 'Revenge is sweet,' Milady thought, and she ran out of the room.

A few minutes later, d'Artagnan ran into the room. 'Constance, I've found you at last!' he cried, taking the young woman in his arms.

'D'Artagnan, is it really you? I can't see you very well! I'm ill!'

D'Artagnan turned to his friends. 'What can I do? Her hands are cold. She's **fainting**! Help me, all of you!'

Athos was looking horrified at the nearly empty wine glass on the table. 'I think there's poison in this glass! Poor woman, poor woman!' he said.

'She's opening her eyes again!' said d'Artagnan.

'Madame, who put the wine in this glass?' asked Athos.

'My dear friend, who's been here with me. Lady de Winter.'

'No!' the musketeers cried out together. At that moment

poison something that kills people when they eat or drink it

faint to fall down suddenly because you are weak, ill, afraid or horrified

Constance's face went grey and she fell from her chair to the ground.

sigh to breathe once, very deeply

'Where are you, d'Artagnan? Hold me! I'm dying!' she cried.

D'Artagnan held her in his arms. 'I'm here, Constance! I'll never leave you! Porthos, Aramis, Athos, get a doctor at once!'

'I'm sorry, d'Artagnan,' said Athos. 'We can't do anything for her now.'

Constance took d'Artagnan's head in her hands and kissed him once, lovingly. Then, with a last **sigh**, she died. D'Artagnan closed his eyes and lay down on the floor next to her.

With a last sigh, she died.

Suddenly a man hurried into the room. 'Gentlemen,' he said, 'I'm Lord de Winter, and, like you, I'm looking for Milady.' He saw the two bodies on the ground. 'Are they both dead?' he asked.

'No,' said Athos. 'D'Artagnan's only fainted.'

Just then d'Artagnan's eyes opened. He took Constance in his arms again, and started crying over her body.

'D'Artagnan, be a man,' said Athos softly. 'Only women cry for the dead. Men take their revenge.'

'I'm with you, if you're planning revenge,' said d'Artagnan.

Athos asked the head of the convent to **arrange** a **funeral** for Madame Bonacieux. Then the five men left the convent, talking about what to do next. Porthos, Aramis, and de Winter wanted to follow Milady at once, to catch her and to punish her. But Athos didn't agree.

'Leave it to me,' he said. 'I'll arrange everything.'

'But I must help you,' said de Winter. 'After all, she is my sister-in-law.'

'And she is my wife,' said Athos, and he quickly told his story. Porthos and Aramis were horrified to hear it. 'There's an inn in this village, so we can stay here tonight,' Athos went on. 'You can safely leave me – Milady's husband – to find her. Oh, d'Artagnan, do you have that piece of paper? You remember, the man from Meung dropped it.'

'Of course!' said d'Artagnan excitedly. 'It has the name of a village on it, in Milady's writing. Here it is.'

The five men went to their bedrooms at the inn, but Athos couldn't sleep. He was planning his attack on Milady. First he called the musketeers' servants to his room, and told them to go to the village of Armentières. Their job was to find out where Milady was staying, and to guard her. Then he put on his sword and **cloak**, and left the inn.

He took the road out of the village into the country. Sometimes he had to ask the way. But at last he arrived at a dark, silent house, and knocked on the door. A tall man with black hair let him in. He lived here alone, with no family or servants, a long way from any other people. Athos sat down and explained what he wanted the man to do. At first the man shook his head. But when Athos showed him the Cardinal's letter, the man thought for a moment, and then agreed. Athos thanked him, and walked back to the inn.

arrange to make a plan for something to happen

funeral the time when a dead person is put under the ground

cloak a coat with no arms

The next day the four friends and de Winter went to Constance's funeral at the convent. Athos told them to be ready to leave that evening. So, at eight o'clock, d'Artagnan, Aramis, Porthos and de Winter were waiting for Athos outside the inn. They were surprised to see Athos ride towards them with another man. He was tall, with a **mask** over his face and wearing a long blue cloak. Nobody asked Athos any questions, and all six of them rode to Armentières.

When they arrived at the village, Planchet took them to a small house near the river. Milady was staying there, and the other servants were on guard duty, in the fields around the house.

With a great shout, Athos broke one of the windows, and jumped through. At the same time d'Artagnan broke down the door, and the others followed him. When she saw them all inside the house, Milady gave a cry, and fell down on to a chair. D'Artagnan lifted his gun and held it to her head.

'Don't shoot, d'Artagnan!' cried Athos. 'We're going to **try** this woman, not murder her!'

mask something that you wear to cover your face

try to ask someone questions to decide if they have done something wrong

'Don't shoot, d'Artagnan!'

'What do you want, all of you?' cried Milady, afraid.

'We want to try you for your crimes,' said Athos, 'and if we decide you are **guilty**, then we'll punish you. D'Artagnan, I call you to speak first!'

D'Artagnan came forward. 'This woman gave poison to Constance Bonacieux, who died yesterday. She tried to kill me three times at La Rochelle, because she hated me!'

'We agree that d'Artagnan's story is all true,' said Porthos and Aramis.

'Now, Lord de Winter, please say something,' said Athos.

'This woman arranged the murder of the Duke of Buckingham. Some years ago she also killed her husband, my brother, with poison!'

'How evil!' cried Porthos and Aramis.

Athos himself now came forward. 'This woman was my wife, until I found out that she was branded!'

Milady jumped up and cried, 'I'm not a criminal! You'll never find the man who branded me! Show me that man, if you can!'

At this, the man in the blue cloak came forward. 'I'm the man who branded you,' he said, taking off his mask.

Milady looked silently at him for a moment. Then she screamed, 'No, it can't be! It's – it's the **executioner** of Lille!'

He turned to the others and explained. 'Yes, I'm the executioner in the town of Lille. This woman was branded, when she was much younger, for a number of evil crimes.'

Now Athos spoke. 'How shall we punish her?' he asked.

'She must die!' said d'Artagnan, and the others all agreed.

'Milady,' said Athos, 'we have found you guilty of your crimes. Get ready to die. If you know how to pray, do it now.'

Milady knew that there was no more hope. The executioner's strong hand fell on her shoulder. Quietly all of them walked out of the little house, and down to the

guilty who has done something wrong

executioner a person whose job is to kill criminals

river. They watched the executioner lift his heavy sword high in the air, and bring it down once on Milady's proud neck. Carefully he put his blue cloak round the dead body, and carried it into the deep water in the middle of the river. The body went down like a stone.

Now that Buckingham was dead, and the war with England was over, the musketeers went back to Paris, where life went on as usual. Sometimes d'Artagnan sighed unhappily over his lost love, but his friends always helped him to feel better.

'There are other pretty women, you know,' smiled Aramis.

'And more adventures for brave musketeers like us!' said Porthos.

'We'll fight for France, and for our King and Queen!' said Athos.

'One for all, and all for one!' they all shouted together.

'One for all, and all for one!'

READING CHECK

What do they say?

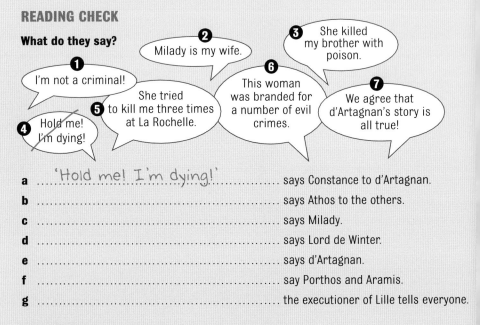

① I'm not a criminal!

② Milady is my wife.

③ She killed my brother with poison.

④ Hold me! I'm dying!

⑤ She tried to kill me three times at La Rochelle.

⑥ This woman was branded for a number of evil crimes.

⑦ We agree that d'Artagnan's story is all true!

a ....'Hold me! I'm dying!'.............. says Constance to d'Artagnan.

b .... says Athos to the others.

c .... says Milady.

d .... says Lord de Winter.

e .... says d'Artagnan.

f .... say Porthos and Aramis.

g .... the executioner of Lille tells everyone.

WORD WORK

Complete the sentences with the pairs of words.

tried   poisoning   ~~fainted   sigh~~   arranged   funeral   cloak   mask   guilty   executioner

a With a deep ...sigh....... Constance died and d'Artagnan .fainted. at once.

b The head of the convent .... Constance's ....

54

c The man from Lille had a .... over his head and he wore a long blue ....

d The musketeers .... Milady for .... her husband and Constance, and for other terrible crimes.

e They decided Milady was .... and the .... of Lille cut off her head.

Project A   *A Diary Page*

1 Read Planchet's diary. Which page of the story does it come from?

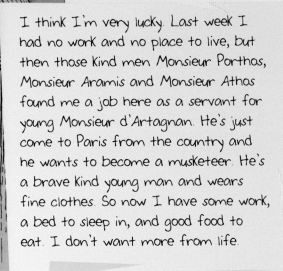

I think I'm very lucky. Last week I had no work and no place to live, but then those kind men Monsieur Porthos, Monsieur Aramis and Monsieur Athos found me a job here as a servant for young Monsieur d'Artagnan. He's just come to Paris from the country and he wants to become a musketeer. He's a brave kind young man and wears fine clothes. So now I have some work, a bed to sleep in, and good food to eat. I don't want more from life.

Yesterday we had a visitor, Monsieur Bonacieux, the owner of our house. He told Monsieur d'Artagnan something interesting. 'Someone's kidnapped my wife!' he said. 'Can you help?' Well, Monsieur d'Artagnan was very interested in that news – a young lady in danger, you know – and now he's going to look for Madame Bonacieux. We had chicken for supper.

2 Put these adjectives into the correct column. Use a dictionary to help you.

PLANCHET

....	brave	....
....	practical	....
....	idealistic	....
....	kind	....
....	romantic	....
....	down-to-earth	....
....	proud	....
....	humble	....

D'ARTAGNAN

3 Complete this page from Planchet's diary.

This morning Monsieur d'Artagnan and his friends decided
they wanted to have a picnic **(a)** ....
I had to carry a basket of **(b)** ....
We walked across **(c)** ....
and then we walked up **(d)** ....
I was very tired when we got there.
During the picnic the English **(e)** ....
The musketeers **(f)** ....
Then the English attacked again, and we pushed
(g) ....
The musketeers weren't afraid, but I **(h)** ....
After the picnic we **(i)** ....

4 Now write another page from Planchet's diary from a different part of the story.

Project B *Past Times*

1 Look at this project on life in England in the 1600s and complete the sentences.

England in the 1600s

a

Oliver Cromwell ruled England from 1653. People asked him to become king but he said 'no'. In 1658 he ....

b

Charles I was king of .... and Scotland from 1625. He thought that kings could do what they wanted without asking parliament.

c

Nell Gwynn was a .... actress and friend of Charles II.

d

In 1660 England brought back **King Charles II** (Charles I's son) who was living in Holland. He was a king who loved pleasure.

Cavaliers and **Roundheads**
From 1642-1649 there was a
Civil War in England between
the long-haired 'cavaliers'
(fighting for the king) and the
short-haired 'roundheads'
(fighting for parliament).
Soldiers fought with ....
and muskets. They rode horses.

John Milton
was a famous poet at this time.
He .... 'Paradise Lost'.

The famous Dutch painter
Van Dyck lived and
.... pictures in
England at this time.

The roundheads won the war and in 1649 the
executioner cut off King Charles I's ....

2 Choose a time in the history of your country and make notes.

Your country:

Time in history:

Rulers

Politics

Wars

Transport

Artists and Writers

Fashion

3 Use your notes to make a project about this time in the history of your country. Use the project on pages 58–59 to help you.

GRAMMAR CHECK

Past Simple: affirmative

We use the Past Simple to talk about things that happened at a specific time in the past and that are now finished.

D'Artagnan's son talked to Monsieur de Tréville.

With regular verbs, we usually add –d/–ed to the infinitive without to.

A young man called d'Artagnan arrived in Paris. He visited Monsieur de Tréville.

With regular verbs that end in consonant + –y, we change the y to i and add –ed.

carry – The musketeers always carried their swords with them.

Some verbs are irregular. You must learn their past forms.

steal – Someone stole two of the Queen's diamonds.

1 Complete d'Artagnan's diary with the Past Simple form of the verbs in brackets.

What an exciting day! First, I a) .....arrived..... (arrive) in the great city of Paris and b) .... (go) to see the Captain of the King's musketeers. I c) .... (tell) him that I wanted to join the musketeers. But suddenly, when I d) .... (look) out of the window, I e) .... (see) the man who f) .... (steal) my father's letter from me at Meung! I g) .... (run) after him. In my hurry, I h) .... (bump) into a musketeer on the stairs, then I i) .... (knock) a second musketeer's hat off by accident and, finally, I j) .... (make) a third man angry by asking about his lady friend! After all that, I k) .... (lose) the man from Meung. Luckily, the three musketeers l) .... (decide) not to fight me, and we m) .... (be) soon good friends. They n) .... (show) me round Paris. And they even o) .... (find) a servant for me! Later, the four of us p) .... (have) dinner together. We q) .... (drink) a lot of good wine, and we r) .... (laugh) at everything that s) .... (happen) today. I think that I'm going to sleep well tonight!

GRAMMAR CHECK

Present Perfect and Past Simple

We use the Present Perfect to talk about things happening at some time in the past without saying when.

I've thought of a plan. Athos hasn't forgotten his wife.

We can also use the Present Perfect to talk about things that began in the past and are continuing now.

I've loved you for a long time. I've never been so happy. (= at no time in my life)

We use the Past Simple to talk about things that happened at a specific time in the past and that are now finished.

One evening last week, the Cardinal met Milady in secret.

2 Complete the Queen's letter. Use the Present Perfect or Past Simple form of the verbs in brackets.

My dear Buckingham,

Do you remember the twelve diamonds that I a) ...gave... (give) you last week? At the time, I b) .... (want) you to have some of my things to keep because I c) .... (not want) you to forget me. But now the King d) .... (explain) to me that there will be an important dinner soon. He e) .... (come) to see me an hour ago and he f) .... (ask) me to wear the diamonds at the dinner! I think that the Cardinal g) .... (speak) to him yesterday and h) .... (tell) him that I have a lover! I i) .... (never/be) so worried before. I must ask you to send back the diamonds.

I know that you and I j) .... (love) each other for years. But all that must stop now. Please burn any letters that I k) .... (write) to you recently, and also this one. I hope that reading this letter I) .... (not make) you too unhappy. Be very careful. Your life is in danger.

Anne

GRAMMAR CHECK

Modal auxiliary verbs: can, can't, must, and mustn't

We use can + infinitive without *to* to talk about things that we are able to do or that are possible.

I can take you to the house of my friend Athos.

We use can't + infinitive without *to* to talk about things that we are not able to do or that are not possible.

We can't talk for long!

We use must + infinitive without *to* when we think it is necessary or very important to do something, or when it is an obligation.

The letter must arrive safely in London.

We use mustn't + infinitive without *to* to talk about things that we think should not happen.

Milady mustn't take her revenge on d'Artagnan.

3 Choose the correct word to complete each sentence.

a D'Artagnan **can't**/**mustn't** keep away from the beautiful Milady.

b Kitty feels that she **must/can** warn d'Artagnan that Milady is evil.

c D'Artagnan thinks that he **can/can't** find out more about Milady from Kitty.

d While he is hiding, d'Artagnan **must/can** hear Milady talking to Kitty.

e When d'Artagnan visits Milady as the Count, she **must/mustn't** know who he really is.

f Athos tells d'Artagnan that the young man **can't/must** forget Milady.

g But d'Artagnan still **mustn't/can't** stop visiting Milady.

h Milady tells d'Artagnan that they **must/can** be happy together.

i Suddenly she attacks him, but she **can't/mustn't** hurt him.

j 'You **must/can** die!' she screams wildly at him.

Negative questions

There are two types of negative question. In the first type, we use can't, won't, don't, or haven't at the beginning of the sentence. Notice the word order for the rest of the question (subject + main verb).

Can't you tell us why, d'Artagnan?   *Won't Lord de Winter arrive in time?*

Don't you love him, Milady?   *Haven't the musketeers won the fight?*

With the verb be, we use isn't, aren't, wasn't, or weren't.

Isn't the servant girl pretty?   *Aren't I brave?*

In the second type of negative question, we start with a question word – usually why – followed by a negative verb.

Why didn't the King notice?   *Why isn't d'Artagnan safe from Milady?*

4 Write the words in the correct order to make questions.

a push / the / can't / enemy / this / on / we / wall / ?

......*Can't we push this wall on the enemy?*......

b they / answer / give / us / can't / the / ?

....

c plan / me / your / you / won't / tell / ?

....

d for / anyone / me / isn't / waiting / ?

....

e aren't / why / married / I / Buckingham / to / ?

....

f Constance / doesn't / and / some / poison / drink / die / ?

....

g had / you / special / England / in / haven't / some / business / ?

....

GRAMMAR CHECK

Question tags

We can use question tags to check information, or to ask someone to agree with us.

The Queen was at the dinner, wasn't she?

This ring's beautiful, isn't it?

The tag contains subject + main verb, or auxiliary verb, to match the sentence.

You were in England then, weren't you?

Constance hasn't been kidnapped, has she?

When the sentence is affirmative, the tag is negative.

Milady is evil, isn't she?

When the sentence is negative, the tag is affirmative.

You won't tell anyone my secret, will you?

5 Complete the sentences with the question tags from the box.

doesn't she	did he	did I	will he	~~aren't I~~	isn't he
won't we	isn't she	wasn't he	haven't they	wasn't I	

a I'm going to become a King's musketeer, *aren't I* ?

b I didn't catch the man from Meung, ... ?

c Buckingham is in love with the Queen, ... ?

d Somebody has stolen the diamonds, ... ?

e The King was angry with the Cardinal, ... ?

f Athos won't fall in love again, ... ?

g Milady's a very beautiful woman, ... ?

h Milady wants to kill me, ... ?

i I was right to say 'no' to the Cardinal, ... ?

j We'll fight the enemy if they attack us, ... ?

k Buckingham didn't seduce Milady, ... ?

GRAMMAR CHECK

Past Continuous and Past Simple with when and while

We use the Past Continuous to talk about longer actions in the past, and the Past Simple to talk about shorter actions in the past.

Athos was running to one of the castle walls.

The five men pushed against the heavy wall.

We use time expressions to show the relationship between two actions in the past. We use while in front of the Past Continuous verb and when in front of the Past Simple verb.

Planchet was resting after the fight when he fell asleep.

While the three friends were talking, Aramis wrote two letters.

6 Complete the sentences. Use the Past Continuous or Past Simple form of the verbs in brackets.

a When d'Artagnan ...*ran*... (run) into the room, Constance *was feeling* (feel) ill.

b She .... (faint) when d'Artagnan .... (ask) his friends for help.

c She .... (find) it very difficult to speak when she .... (say) the name of Lady de Winter.

d While she .... (die), she .... (call) for d'Artagnan.

e She .... (give) him a loving kiss while she .... (lie) in his arms.

f While this .... (happen), Lord de Winter .... (hurry) into the room.

g While d'Artagnan .... (cry) over Constance's dead body, Athos .... (try) to make him feel better.

h When the four friends .... (leave) the room, they .... (talk) about what to do next.

i While they .... (make) their plans, Athos .... (tell) them that Milady was his wife.

GRAMMAR CHECK

Reported speech with say and explain

In direct speech we give the words that people say.	In reported speech, we begin with that, put the verb one step into the past, and change the pronouns and possessive adjectives.
'I love a young man called d'Artagnan,' said Milady.	*Milady said that she loved a young man called d'Artagnan.*
'D'Artagnan, I can give you a job,' said the Cardinal.	*The Cardinal explained that he could give d'Artagnan a job.*

Note that *now* becomes *then* in reported speech.

7 Write the sentences again. Use reported speech.

a 'I want to kill Milady now!' said d'Artagnan.

<u>D'Artagnan said that he wanted to kill Milady then.</u>

b 'We agree with you, Athos,' said Porthos and Aramis.

....

c 'Milady never stops trying to kill me!' said d'Artagnan.

....

....

d 'She's a branded criminal,' Athos explained.

....

....

e 'I know you, and you're evil,' said the executioner to Milady.

....

f 'We find you guilty, Milady,' Athos explained.

....

g 'I don't want to die so young!' said Milady.

....

h 'You can pray, if you like,' Athos said to Milady.

....

DOMINOES Your Choice

Read *Dominoes* for pleasure, or to develop language skills. It's your choice.

Each *Domino* reader includes:
- a good story to enjoy
- integrated activities to develop reading skills and increase vocabulary
- task-based projects – perfect for CEFR portfolios
- contextualized grammar activities

Each *Domino* pack contains a reader, and an excitingly dramatized audio recording of the story

If you liked this *Domino*, read these:

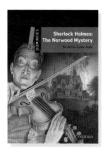

Sherlock Holmes: The Norwood Mystery
Sir Arthur Conan Doyle

'For me, Watson, life is not so interesting,' says Holmes. 'I loved to read the newspaper, hoping to find some news of an interesting crime for me to investigate or a dangerous criminal for me to catch. Where are all those clever criminals these days?'

Then, suddenly, a wild, excited young man runs up the stairs to Holmes' room. He has a story to tell about a strange crime that took place in Norwood. But who is the criminal? And is he dangerous? Life, for Holmes, suddenly starts to get interesting.

Lord Arthur Savile's Crime and Other Stories
Oscar Wilde

The three stories in this book are about ordinary people, people like you and me; but they find themselves in surprising situations. Lord Arthur Savile, a rich man with no enemies, finds out that he must do something terrible before he can marry. Poor young Hughie Erskine gives money to an old beggar – but the beggar is not what he seems. And Lord Murchison falls in love with a mystery woman – but what is the strange secret behind the door in Cumnor Street?

	CEFR	Cambridge Exams	IELTS	TOEFL iBT	TOEIC
Level 3	B1	PET	4.0	57-86	550
Level 2	A2–B1	KET-PET	3.0-4.0	–	390
Level 1	A1–A2	YLE Flyers/KET	3.0	–	225
Starter & Quick Starter	A1	YLE Movers	1.0–2.0	–	–

You can find details and a full list of books and teachers' resources on our website:
www.oup.com/elt/gradedreaders